# God Is for Real, Man

# God Is for Real, Man

*Interpretations of
Bible passages and stories,
as told by some of God's bad-tempered
angels with busted halos to*

## Carl F. Burke

Chaplain of Erie County Jail
Buffalo, New York

ASSOCIATION PRESS • NEW YORK

*To Caroline, my wife*

First Printing    –    February 1966
Second Printing   –    May 1966
Third Printing    –    July 1966
Fourth Printing   –    August 1966
Fifth Printing    –    September 1966
Sixth Printing    –    November 1966
Seventh Printing  –    April 1967
Eighth Printing   –    October 1967

**GOD IS FOR REAL, MAN**

*Copyright © 1966 by*

*National Board of Young Men's Christian Associations*

Association Press, 291 Broadway, New York, N. Y. 10007

*Publisher's stock number: 1612p, paper; 1609, cloth
Library of Congress catalog card number: 66-15746*

**PRINTED IN UNITED STATES OF AMERICA**

*I simply argue that the cross be raised again at the center of the marketplace as well as on the steeple of the church. I am recovering the claim that Jesus was not crucified in a cathedral between two candles, but on a cross between two thieves; on the town garbage heap; at a crossroad so cosmopolitan that they had to write his title in Hebrew and in Latin and in Greek . . . at the kind of place where cynics talk smut, and thieves curse, and soldiers gamble. Because that is where he died. And that is what he died about. And that is where churchmen ought to be, and what church-men should be about.*

GEORGE MACLEOD

# Contents

GOD IS FOR REAL, MAN    • **8**

## How This Book Came to Be

"Mister, what's God like?" That's the question that started this book. It was asked several years ago on a trail leading to the campfire circle at Camp Vick, the Western New York Baptist Camp. The answer to the seemingly simple question came without the slightest hesitation, and with the authority of a theological education, plus several years' experience as a pastor, and above all, with the confidence that was expected of an "adult leader." "God," was the answer, "is like a father."

The reply from the boy came slowly and devastated the adult leader, his experience, his theological education, and the confidence that is expected of an "adult leader." "Hah," the boy said with much venom, "if he's like my father I sure would hate him." The rest of the trip to the fire circle was made in silence. The "adult leader" was never the same again.

Try this one. An eight-year-old girl, abandoned on the streets of a large city, asks, "If God loves me like you say he does, why did he let Mommy and Daddy go away on me?" If you try to answer this, remember that you are speaking to an eight-

year-old who has never experienced parental love
—a girl who has known little of family relationships except that she is not really a child—she is
an intrusion.

Or what about a boy whose parents are "winos"
or "junkies," or a combination of both? He asks
about honoring your father and mother. There is,
of course, a Christian answer to this. The problem
is, how do you verbalize it? How do you talk of
the love of a father to a boy whose concept of a
father is that of a "drunken bum" who often
wakes lying in his own vomit and who fails to
provide for his children? How does one honor
him? Or, when the same thing applies to a mother
and some of "her men," where do honor and
respect come in? Honor, respect, love: for many
of the children who have shared in the writing of
this book these are merely words that have no
meaning in demonstrable concepts.

What does the servant of Jesus Christ do when
all the forms of his middle-class society and
family relationships, and even the meaning of
words, are stripped from him? Does he ignore it
with the hope that this nightmare will go away,
or that he will be transferred to a nice quiet par-
ish? Is he helpless? I think not!

The children of the inner city, these young
"angels with busted halos," who are the co-
authors of this book, are the victims of a paradox.
The goals of our churches are completely foreign

to them. Portraying "the American dream of un-limited opportunity" we talk about wealth, status and education, and a God who loves us and cares for us.

At the same time we deny the children of the inner city — and their parents, sometimes — a chance to achieve these goals. Many have little contact with anything successful; frustrated, they seek to establish their own goals. They seek to establish their own system of values and group-ings, and even of religion. Status may depend on fights, flouting authority, and stealing. Beyond it all, there is still that cry for help and a desire to know God, but not according to the forms of a church that seemingly has already deserted them, holds out goals they cannot reach, and speaks words they do not understand.

This book represents a search for a way in which spiritual truths can be taught in frames of reference that are real and vivid, in language and thought patterns that are understood, and that have meaning. It is an attempt to permit the so-called inner city adolescent to speak to us, rather than us to him, and "that's a switch."

Some, no doubt, will find this book amusing. It was done in almost deadpan seriousness. Some will find it a novelty. It was not intended as such. No doubt some will find it repulsive, and border-ing on heresy. It is this author's high calling to work with youth who have unique spiritual needs that have not been met by conventional methods. Must we give up because a method is unorthodox? I think not, I cannot, I will not!

There is nothing new in this method. It is as old as the first missionaries who found language barriers. It is permitting the children and youth to paraphrase in their own terms and thought-patterns the Bible stories that are familiar to us. The only rule that must be observed is to keep the basic meaning of the message being taught in the Bible. Missionaries are still doing it.

As you read this book, listen to what is being said. Do you hear the call for help of the little boy who worked at the Twenty-third Psalm (The Lord Is Like My Probation Officer . . .")? Do you feel the strong desire to "change a way of life" in the parable of the talents ("If Ya Use Your Brains They Grow")? In other paraphrases, can you sense the frustrations, the feeling of hope-lessness, and yet an underlying expression that here at last maybe there is hope, just maybe?

These children are not all knife fighters or hoodlums that make the headlines, though some of them are. They are the ones caught in pressures with which they cannot cope. They are the unwanted children of irresponsible parents. They are children who are becoming . . . what we help them to become.

A word to those who may try to make the meaning of the Bible come alive by bringing its

GOD IS FOR REAL, MAN

messages into the everyday vocabulary and experience of such youth: For every productive session there will be many unproductive sessions. Biblical paraphrasing cannot be forced. It must be natural and it must arise out of a natural situation. The author has not found a specific technique or formula which works each time when a paraphrasing project is attempted. Perhaps an illustration or two will help to answer questions.

For instance, "A Cool Square Comes to the Rescue" came about in the following manner. We were sitting in a detention home, engaged in some trivial conversation, when one of the boys dropped, quite accidentally, a part of a model airplane that he was building. It rolled a considerable distance from him under the chair of another boy. The boy who dropped it asked the other boy to pick it up and toss it over to him. The reply was, "Why the hell should I?" This opened an opportunity to discuss why we might be able to help others or to "give another guy a break." This in turn led me to bring in the parable of the Good Samaritan. The boys then talked about how a somewhat similar situation might have happened in a twentieth-century setting.

The version of the Twenty-third Psalm, "The Lord Is Like My Probation Officer . . . ," was done by one boy and myself. The young lad was the victim of what psychologists call a "rejection syndrome." He was quite convinced that no one in the world had the slightest interest in him, and he expressed a longing for someone to whom he could turn. We were seeking for something that would have meaning to him. About the only one he could think of who had shown interest in him was the Probation Officer, for whom he had great admiration. Thus, by our working together, this boy was able to express his feelings and establish a relationship with a person, which he could then translate into a relationship with our Lord.

Some of the paraphrases in this book are exactly as the youngsters worded them. Some are simply the author's recalling to mind as nearly as possible that which has been discussed over several years. Sometimes the children or youth wrote them out. Sometimes they dictated them, and at other times it was only a discussion of which no written record was kept. Their grammar has been retained, but misspellings have been corrected in most cases because there were so many that it would be almost impossible for the reader to recognize the intended words.

Words mean different things to different groups, and their meanings change from time to time. If a word or a phrase does not seem to make sense, the reader may consult the glossary at the end of the book. The more generally familiar slang terms, however, such as "fairy," "hideout," "hootenanny," are not included in the list.

It is well to remember that the effort to paraphrase must start with the youngsters, not with the adult. The adult is there only in a guiding or prompting role.

Some of the paraphrases in this book are extreme in their use of slang; others have nearly middle-class speech patterns. The reason for this variation is that the work of paraphrasing was done over several years and by different age groups as well as by groups from various backgrounds: some in a jail or detention home setting, some at a summer camp, and others in the released-time program of a city church. All the paraphrases possess one thing in common—they represent young people in need of God's love and care. To use a cliché heard many, many times, they are "souls for whom Christ died."

THE OLD TESTAMENT offers a number of stories that can be used to teach children concepts of God and his concern for others, but, more to the point, how to handle some of the problems of life. Many of them are too long for direct paraphrasing, or too involved, or seemed too preposterous, such as Daniel in the lion's den or Jonah in the whale. These are quickly rejected by inner city children as "gassers."

The following are examples of certain stories that were reduced to language and situations that made some sense to these youngsters. The story of the Flood was accepted as a story that could have happened. The Moses and Pharaoh incident was introduced naturally when some boys were talking about two men in the neighborhood who were "always fighting and doing rotten things to each other." The boys were interested in this somewhat similar feud in the Bible and in how God had worked through it. It was difficult to separate the sexual from the Samson and Delilah story. You will note the "out to make her." The same was true with the story of Jonathan and David, whom they considered as two "queers."

Once these problems were faced and worked with, we could go on to talk about friendship and the love of God, and how God sometimes works through just such incidents as the Old Testament describes and even through the unpleasant experiences of the present day.

# The Story of the Cool Cat Called Noah

The Forty-Day Flood (Genesis 6-9)

One day God was looking over the world he made, but things was a mess. Seemed like there was gangs on every corner—maybe rumbles and things like that. Nobody paid much attention to God—in fact they didn't even think about him and, if they did—which they didn't very much anyway—they just didn't care. Churches didn't make that much difference then, either.

Well—God tried all kinds of ways to get them to settle down. Nothing happened. Everybody just kept on yelling. God was bugged that he even thought of making the world. So there was only one thing to do—throw the whole damn thing out and start again. But he had worked too hard to throw everything away, in that Creation bit, and he didn't want to go through that again.

He found a cool cat called Noah. He was a golden-ager like at the Salvation Army. God told Noah to build a boat—a big one, no little rowboat —so he did.

Everybody came by and poked fun at him— they yelled dirty words at him—they thought he was a nut or a Holy Roller. But that didn't make no never mind for Noah and his kids—they just made the boat.

Noah tried to tell the people to knock it off or they would be sorry—but they didn't, and were they ever sorry later, like crazy they were!

So one day Noah took two animals and snakes and birds of every kind (boys and girls, that is) on his boat which he named Ark.

Sure enough! God was right and so was Noah—it did rain—Geez, didn't it rain forty days and nights—there was a flood—no wonder, huh?

Pretty soon the boat started to move but nobody said bon voyage—they were yellin', "Let me in." But Noah said, "Too late—you too late." And they were, 'cause they all got drowned.

After forty days Noah let a bird fly out the window, but it came back—all the ledges on the buildings were flooded and the bird couldn't find a place to set down. Pretty soon the bird went out again and came back with a leaf from an elm tree. "Ah ha!" says Noah. "Land's back," and he tells the gang of animals, "Next week ya can all go"—and, boy, were they glad to get off.

Noah was so glad he made like a shrine like you see at St. Bridget's, and later he got stoned.

Then God said, "All right, you guys, let that be a lesson to you. This hurt me more than it hurt you, and I ain't never gonna do that again."

So instead of tying a string around his finger to remind him never to do it again, he made a rainbow.

So every time you see a rainbow you better hope God don't forget, and don't you, either. And if you do you just better know how to swim, man.

GOD IS FOR REAL, MAN

## Moses' Big War Plan

The Story of Moses and Pharaoh (Exodus 8-12)

Moses' people were P.W.'s in Egypt.

Moses goes to a guy named Pharaoh to try to get the people cut free. But it was no go with that Pharaoh 'cause something was always bugging him. So Moses and his lieutenant Aaron cooks up a big war plan with the help of God. It was real wild.

You don't haveta believe it if you don't want to, but this is what it was like. First, Moses and his war counselor put a stick over the river. Billions of frogs came hopping out. They got all over the road, and cars ran over them making a mess. They got in people's cribs and in the pots on the stove, in people's pockets. You name it, and those damn frogs were there. Pharaoh gets mad and calls in a couple of spookers and tells them to use their magic to get rid of them, but it don't work— just makes more frogs. Pharaoh gets real worried about this, so he sends for Moses and Aaron and says, "All right, you guys, so you win. Call off the frogs and I'll cut out your people." So Moses and the war counselor calls off the frogs. Well, Pharaoh don't learn so fast, and when the frogs are all dead he turns turkey and don't let the people go.

So Moses and Aaron says, "OK, wise guy, how about this one? Maybe this will make you do what you promise." So they hit the dust at the curb with their stick—and the street is full of bedbugs, cockroaches, and ticks. Pharaoh's spookers try to call them off, but they couldn't do it. So Pharaoh says, "No go again."

The next day Moses and Aaron tells him, "You better give in, man, or you'll see more flies than you knew there was." But he didn't give in. Then the flies came—billions and billions of them. They got into people's ears and eyes, on their food and everywhere you can think of. There was one place they didn't get—that was in the cribs of Moses' people. Pharaoh calls Moses and says, "I'll make a deal with you. Your people can go, but they gotta stay where we can keep an eye on them." Moses says, "Nothin' doin'. Your people may kill my people when we ain't lookin'."

This Pharaoh is mighty hard to get along with. He makes a hard deal and nothin' moves him. To try to soften him up, all the cows out on the farms get sick, and so there's no milk to put in the slot machines on the corner. That don't make him move either. Then everybody gets boils. That don't make no difference—he just puts black salve on them. Then comes a big storm with thunder and lightning, but, worst of all, hail comes. Great big hail things that bust the windows and hurt when they hit you in the head. Lots of people and the cows gets killed. But he still don't give in. He just makes out that he is gonna, so that the storm will stop.

Next comes a big bunch of bugs that eats up everything. Well, Pharaoh's own people are getting sick of this now and they tells him, "How about getting this rumble settled? We're sick of it."

So Pharaoh tries to make another deal. He says, "I'll tell you what. You can go, but leave the men here." That's no good to Moses, so he don't fall for it. Pharaoh tries again. You gotta admit he tries hard. This time he says, "How about you and your people goin', but leave your cows and things here?" Moses says, "That's out too." And you gotta admit that Moses don't give in easy either. Now old Pharaoh gets real mad and yells, "Get out of my life, beat it, get lost, scram, and if you ever come back here again I'll personally kill the bunch of ya." Moses says, "The feelings the same. Drop dead."

Then one more thing happened just to make sure that Pharaoh don't change his mind 'cause you can't trust him. The oldest cat in each family died. That did it. This time Pharaoh and his people made sure that Moses and his people did go. Funny thing about the oldest cats in each family dying. None of Moses' people did. They put some blood on the door, and that took care of it just like when you get a shot at school. That's what made the black angel pass over Moses' people. After that, Moses and his people started on their long trip back to their own turf.

# God Is Mr. Big, Real Big

Interpretations of The Ten Commandments
(Exodus 20:3-17)

1. *You shall have no other gods before me. . . .* \*
   Means God's the leader—nobody, but no-body, man, gets in the way.
   This is the top. He is Mr. Big, real big.

2. *You shall not make for yourself a graven image. . . .*
   This means no making things that look like God in the craftshop at the settlement house. No worship things like rabbits' foots and lucky dice and, damn it, dolls.

3. *You shall not take the name of the Lord your God in vain. . . .*
   It means knock off the swearing, or you better watch out.

4. *Observe the Sabbath day, to keep it holy. . . .*
   a. It means going to church on Sunday and listen to people who don't know much about what they are talking about.
   b. Keeping it holy means no snatching purses on Sunday.

*Scripture quotations throughout this publication are from the *Revised Standard Version of the Bible,* copyrighted 1946 and 1952 by the Division of Christian Education, National Council of Churches, and used by permission.

    c. Means: Taking a rest on Sunday—like
       my old man not feeling bad 'cause he
       can't find a job and loafing around at the
       gin mill.

5. *Honor your father and your mother.*
    a. It means no calling your father a wino or
       your mother the old lady, even if they are.
    b. It means to love your mother, even if she
       hollers at you, and try to understand she
       is tired from working all day. It means
       to try to love your father, even if you
       don't know him or where he is.
    c. Maybe the others are OK, but this one is
       a real gasser—honor my father and mother
       —to hell with that, man!

6. *You shall not kill....*
    a. No holding up people with switch blades.
    b. No playing chicken in the freight yards.
    c. No real rough fighting.

7. *Neither shall you commit adultery....*
    a. No messing around with the girls in the
       park.
    b. No whoring around.

8. *Neither shall you steal....*
    That's it, don't need to say more.
    Why not? Everybody does it.

9. *Neither shall you bear false witness. . . .*

No telling lies to the cops or in court, no matter how many breaks they say they'll give you.

10. *Neither shall you covet. . . .*

    a. Stop being so sorry for yourself and always wanting something you ain't got. (Feeling sorry only takes up time when you could be shining shoes to earn money to get the things you covet.)

    b. You ain't supposed to do it—but it's not so bad if it makes you try hard to get something you ain't got—if you don't get it by shoplifting.

# How Come You So Strong, Samson?

The Story of Samson and Delilah (Judges 16:4-31)

Samson knew that the Philistines hated his guts. But he knew too that they didn't dare beat up on him. 'Cause he was the war man from his gang. Samson was in love with a broad named Delilah and was out to make her. So he went on the Philistines' turf whenever he wanted.

When the Pres of the Philistines got on to this he figured a way to get Samson. The Pres and the war counselor goes over to see Delilah and tells her, "Broad, you find out how come this cat's so strong and how to make him weak, and we'll pay you a real stack of dough."

So Delilah starts to think of all the things she could get with the dough—a house, and a car, and a big steak dinner, and all that kind of crap. Then she figures that she is the doll of the Philistines anyway and she might's well play along, and anyway that's a nice stack of dough that they are talking about. So she says, "It's a deal."

The next time Samson shows up at her pad Delilah says, "Hey, man, how come you so strong?" But he didn't tell her, he just tells her a way he could show off how strong he is.

He says, "If you tie me with a rope seven times I would be the same as anyone else." Delilah waits till Samson is asleep and then runs and tells the Pres about it. They tie him up while he is asleep.

Then Delilah yells, "Hey, man, wake up." He looks at the rope and laughs and breaks it without half trying. Then Delilah gets mad and says, "Man, how come you poke fun at me? Come on, baby, tell me how come you so strong?"

Then Samson tried a new trick to lead her on and says, "You used old rope that ain't so strong. If you use a new one I couldn't do it and I would be just like anyone else." So the broad don't learn so fast and she tried the same trick again. And Samson does the same bit again and busts the new rope. Delilah gets mad, but she don't give up. Who would when there's that kind of dough around? Then the next time Samson comes cruising in the Philistines' pad Delilah tries again. She says, "Samson baby, be nice to your honey child and tell me how come you so strong?" He leads her on again and tells her, "If you braid my beatle hair I'll lose all my strength." That sounds pretty stupid too, but she tries. But Samson gets out of it just like he knew he would.

Do you think Delilah gave up then? Nothin' doin', that dough's still there and she's out to get it. This time she really turns it on and gets real close to Samson and says, "Come on, man, tell your little baby Delilah how come you so strong?" Well, Samson he's gettin' tired of this crap now. But when Delilah looks up in his face with them great big eyes he can't hold out no more and he tells her the truth. He tells her that all the people

GOD IS FOR REAL, MAN

in the Nazarite gang are strong because their hair's never been cut. If it gets cut he won't be strong no more. Delilah thinks this sounds kinda screwy, but she goes along with it anyway. She cuts his hair when he is asleep. Then she yells, "Hey, man, the Philistines are here." Samson wakes up, and sure enough his hair is gone and so is his strength. The Philistines get their man, and Delilah gets her dough. Then the Philistines put Samson to work for them grinding grain in the flour mills. So that Samson won't get away they made him blind. All the time Samson's hair was growing back, and so was his strength. Then one day the Philistines' cats wanted to have some fun and they thought that they would poke fun at Samson. A kid brought him to the center of the Mall 'cause he couldn't see. This was a good chance for Samson to get even with the Philistines. So he got hold of the posts on the apartments and gave a big heave—bingo, down comes the whole damn thing and killed all the Philistines, and it served them right!

## God Is Still the Boss

The Story of David and Goliath (I Samuel 17)

There was a gang called Philistines who were planning a rumble with a gang called Israelites. The big men got together and picked out the turf. It was between two big hills. The Phils set up on one—the Israelites on the other.

The Phils had a big cat who was always shootin' off his mouth. He yelled over to the Israelites, "I can go up on any cat you got over there. We'll make a deal with you cats—send some cat over to go up on me if you got one with heart. If he kills me we're your slaves. If I kill him you're our slaves." He was such an old blow-hard he agreed to a fair one.

When the Israel gang saw him he was bigger than a football player. He was a giant. They saw his tools—switchblade and zip gun—and when they heard his loud voice a-bellowing, they all chickened out, but quick.

This giant cat never did knock it off. He yelled every A.M. and every P.M. Always the same thing —"Come on out and I'll go up on you." But no Israelite cat would leave his pad and cross the lines. They weren't that much of a nut. This goes on for forty days and nights. Still no cat to go up on him. There is no guy to get proved.

While this was happening there is a little cat named David, home taking care of his old man's pad. He has three brothers that's in the Israelite gang. The old man fixes up a package for them. He puts some apples and bread and fags in and tells David to go give it to his brothers. Sent along a bottle of beer for Mr. Big (that's the Israelite gang's chief). David is supposed to bribe the big man to find out how his brothers are and then come back and tell his old man.

When David got to the rumble turf he saw that some of the gang were scared. So David said, "What's the matter with you guys? I thought you said you could take them?" Then one of the Israelites said to David, "Cool it, man, ain't you seen that giant?" David says, "To hell with him —I'll take him myself."

The Israelites tried to tell David how big the giant was but he still said, "To hell with him."

One of David's brothers didn't like this, 'cause it made him look like a chicken. He was mad.

David says, "So what did I do?"

David got taken to Mr. Big. He looked him over but he figured David was just a kid and can't do nothing and just laughed at him.

But David tells him about how he can take care of himself, so the big cat cays, "OK, what the hell, the kid's got to learn sometime and get some experience." So he gives him his zip and other armor. But David says, "I got my own method."

Then he starts after Goliath (that's the giant's name). Everybody's watching this one.

David gets some smooth rocks and puts them in his pocket. Then he takes out his slingshot he made himself out of an old inner tube and goes looking for the giant.

The giant sees David coming and just laughs and laughs, but he's really mad. He thinks the Israelites are poking fun at him by sending the kid after him. "Hey, kid," he yells, "what you think I am—a little pup or something? I'll knock your teeth in with my thumb."

David can yell too, so he yells back, "I ain't afraid of you, big man, 'cause the Lord's on my side." This makes the giant think this kid's a religious nut or something. David says, "When I get through with you every cat will know that God is still the boss in all the pads."

So the giant starts toward David yelling and swearing. David puts a rock in his sling. Takes good aim. Whomp! Right between the eyes and Goliath fell down conked out. The priest come and give him last rites.

So the Philistine gang knows when they are licked and beat it out of there quick-like.

But the Israelite gang is very high 'cause they know that David's right. God's got 'em switched on.

## Pals to the End

The Story of Jonathan and David (I Samuel 20)

This is a story about two squeaks named David and Jonathan who were good friends, but their parents didn't like it. Jonathan's old man didn't like David and was gonna kill him.

One day David says to Jonathan, "How come your old man wants to kill me? I ain't done nothin to hurt him."

This is news to Jonathan and he says, "What you talkin about, man? You must be some kind of a nut. My old man don't want to kill you—what you want to say that for?" David don't like saying so, but he knows he better watch out for this kid's old man or he won't be watching nothin' 'cause he will be dead. So Jonathan says, "I'm telling ya, Dave, he won't hurt ya, and if he was mad at ya he'd tell me not to hang around with ya."

Just to be on the safe side Jonathan tells Dave, "If the old man says anything about ya I'll tell ya, 'cause you're my buddy boy; then you can get out of his way." So they makes a deal on it and shakes hands.

The next day was a big party at Jonathan's house and his old man would be expectin' David to come. But you ain't gettin' David there for nothin' ya can give him. He ain't gettin' killed if he can help it, and he can, so he don't make no plans to go there. He tells Jonathan to tell his old man that. Jonathan said it was OK for him to go and be with his family in another town for the big party. They figures that if Jonathan's old man, whose name is Saul, gets mad it will prove that he's out to get him. So Jonathan buys that and says that Dave can go for three days. David says, "OK, thanks, pal, but we got one problem. How we gonna know what your old man says when he finds out I ain't there?" So they worked out a plan. When Dave gets back he will hide behind a rock. Jonathan will shoot three of his arrows up in the air like he was shooting at a target. Then he would send a little cat out to get them. He will make like he don't know that Dave's there. If he yells at the little cat the arrows is on the other side. Dave would know that old Saul ain't mad at him and ain't gonna do nothin' to him. But if he yells that the arrows are still far up in the field he would know that old Saul is pretty mad and he better get out before he gets killed 'cause the old man ain't foolin' around. They figured if Saul was gonna kill Dave he might put a tail on Jonathan, and this way he could tell Dave without the old man knowing anything about it. Pretty smart, huh!

So Dave went. While the feast was on, Saul is playing it cool. He knows that Dave's not there but he don't say nothin' about it. Maybe he's sick, or somethin' like that happened, is what he makes off he was thinkin'. Then the next day Dave's still not there. This time old Saul gets suspicious that maybe something ain't right so he says to Jonathan, "Where your pal, Dave?" Jonathan tells his old man where Dave's gone and that he said OK for him to go. Oh, boy, does this make Saul mad! Saul asks Jonathan, "How come you did that? You stay away from that kid. I don't want you playing with him. I'm gonna kill him when I get my hands on him. Then you will be king some day, and not that no good brat." Jonathan starts to play it cool now and he says, "Pa, how come you want to kill him? He ain't done nothin' bad." This gets Saul really jumpin' and he throws a big stick at his son, Jonathan. That did it, now he knows.

This gets Jonathan mad, and he runs away from the table and he won't eat his food and he's mad at his old man for what he said about his pal. He even thought about running away from home. He couldn't do that 'cause the next day is when they had to put their plan to work. So the next day comes, and Dave gets back from visiting his own family and hides behind the rock. Pretty soon Jonathan comes with a little cat just like he said he would. That's 'cause pals always keep the promises that they make to each other. David was glad that Jonathan didn't turn turkey about it. Then Jonathan shoots the arrow just like he said he would, and it goes right over the little cat's head and Jonathan yells, "It way over there—go get it." That's the signal, and David knows he was right and that old Saul is mad at him and gonna kill him. The little cat gets the arrows and brings them back, but he don't know what's up. Jonathan tells him to be a good cat and take them home for him. He did.

As soon as the little cat was gone Dave came out of hiding. Dave was very glad to have the warning, so he shook Jonathan's hand and says, "Thanks, pal." They made a deal that they would always be friends and when they grew up and had kids the kids would be friends too and they would make sure of that.

Then Dave beat it out of there while he was still alive; and his pal to the end, Jonathan, went home to live with his old man.

GOD IS FOR REAL, MAN

THE WRITER OF THE PSALMS spoke of his relationship to God and of his confidence in God in terms of his everyday experience and surroundings: hence, "The Lord is my Shepherd," "I will lift up my eyes unto the hills," and many other personal experiences. In their paraphrases, the children of the city do the very same thing. For Joe, his "shepherd" is the Probation Officer; his "valley of the shadow of death" is a drunken mother who neglects him; and his protector is not the shepherd with his staff, but the Probation Officer with the authority of a court. Hills are something that is seldom seen, but "high risers" are as common to urban children as the hills were to David.

There can be little doubt that behind these words there is still the longing to know God and to find protection in this "valley of tears" or this "lousy, stinking world."

# A Guy Is Pretty Smart . . .

Psalm 1

A guy is pretty smart
  If he don't hang around with hoods
    And do what they tell him.

He is smart too if he don't poke fun
  At people who try to do the right thing.

He is always happy 'cause he knows for sure
  That he is doing the right thing.

In fact it makes him feel so good
  That he thinks about it day and night,
    And that don't do no harm either.

He feels good 'cause this is God's way of doing things,
  And you can't beat that.

This guy is sort of like a tree
  In Humboldt Park
    That grows by the lake.

It don't get looking like a droop
  'Cause it gets plenty of water
    And things to live from.

But the hoods are not like that—
  They are like the dust that blows down the street
    And all over the place,
      And ya hate it.

So they won't stand a chance.
   When the day comes to figure out the score
      They will just get wiped up
         And they won't be where the good guys
         are—
            And that's for sure too.

That's 'cause God knows the way
   People are
      Down inside of them,
         And you can't give him a snow job.

A hood may be on top now,
   But it won't last.

## The Lord Is Like My Probation Officer . . .

Psalm 23

The Lord is like my Probation Officer,
   He will help me,
      He tries to help me make it every day.
         He makes me play it cool
            And feel good inside of me.

He shows me the right path
   So I'll have a good record,
      And he'll have one too.

Because I trust him,
   And that ain't easy,
      I don't worry too much about
         What's going to happen.
            Just knowing he cares about
               Me helps me.

He makes sure I have my food
   And that Mom fixes it.
      He helps her stay sober
         And that makes me feel good
            All over.

He's a good man, I think,
   And he is kind;
      And these things will stay
         With me.

And when I'm kind and good
   Then I know the Lord
      Is with me like the Probation Officer.

GOD IS FOR REAL, MAN

# God Is a Good Hideout . . .

God is a good hideout,
He is stronger than the weight lifter at the Y.
He helps you out even when you got trouble,
So what have you got to worry about even if
there's a flood,
And the streets go caving in, and bridges get
washed out?

When the creek is low it's easy to see how pretty
it is
And that God is there.
But he is there when the creek's mad too.
When the going gets rough, just remember that
God is with us
Like he was with guys of old.

So take a look around—there's nice things—
As well as dirty empty lots and wrecked buildings.
Sometimes it's quiet-like at the end of a rumble.

So take time to think and you'll know about
God—
And that he is here most of the time.

# I Will Look Above the High Risers . . .

Psalm 121

I will look above the high risers.
  If I wants to find some help,
    It comes from God who made everything.

He won't let you get pushed around.
  He won't go to sleep on you
    And he will always be interested in you.

God is the kind of father
  That you wished you had.

No one can sneak up on you when he is around
  Either in the day or in the night
    Or when the street light's busted.

He will keep the big kids
  From beatin' on you,
    And they won't hurt you with him around.

God watches over you
  Every place you go
    And for all your life.

AS A GENERAL RULE, "angels with busted halos" have rejected the adult world. For them most adult advice has been only "gas" given by parents who reject them or by adults whose only object is to use them for the gain. Thus it is not easy to interest the youngsters in the Book of Proverbs, even though it contains many words of wisdom that could assist the young people of the city streets if it were accepted and understood.

The examples given represent an attempt to put some of these words into the thought-patterns and experiences of city children. The wisdom was not always taken nor heeded, but then neither is this done by the average church youth.

For the sake of easy comparison we are using in many cases Revised Standard Version in italics, followed by the paraphrase.

# Don't Be a Lazy Bum

Advice to the Sluggard (Proverbs 6:6-19)

Take a look at the ants on the sidewalk.
   Think about how they work
      And you'll be with it, man.

They don't got a worker to
   Check up on them—right!

They gets their own food
   Then puts it away till they needs it.
      Don't need no government surplus stuff.

So don't be a lazy bum
   And sleep all day—
      Get up and go shine shoes.

Sleep's a good thing at night,
   But too much is too much—
      And a lazy cat ends up
         on welfare—
            It just sneaks up on you.

A lazy guy
   Is like a hood—
      You can't believe anything
         He says.

He's got shifty pincers,
   Always blaming someone
      For his troubles,
         Always trying to con a guy
            And stirring up trouble.

Then before he knows what happened
  Bingo—
    It's too late to straighten up.

There are six things that are
  No go with God:
      1. Shifty pincers
      2. Con artists
      3. Hands that are always
        Beating up on someone
      4. An operator who thinks up a job
      5. A stool pigeon
      6. A cat who stirs up trouble.

These kind of guys are "no go" with God.

# Playing It Cool

How to Keep Out of a Fight (Proverbs 15:1-7)

Playing it cool
   Will keep you out of a fight without losing face.

But shooting your mouth off
   Will get another guy all teed up,
      And he will climb all over you.

Sometimes what a square says may be right
   And he may know something.
      It might be a good idea to listen.

A hood is always sounding off,
   Mostly about things he don't know anything
   about.

God is everywhere keeping watch
   And he is ready to help you.

But a fool don't pay no attention—
   He thinks
      Nobody knows anything but him.

*The fear of the Lord is the beginning of*
*knowledge;*
*fools despise wisdom and instruction*
(Proverbs 1:7).

Trusting God is the first step in getting wised up
And only some kind of a nut
Don't want to learn new things.

\* \* \*

*My son, if sinners entice you,*
*do not consent* (Proverbs 1:10).

Even if the gang calls you chicken, don't give in.

\* \* \*

*Hear, O sons, a father's instruction,*
*and be attentive, that you may*
*gain insight* (Proverbs 4:1).

You better listen to what your old man is saying; maybe he's right, you may learn something.

\* \* \*

*Put away from you crooked speech,*
*and put devious talk far from you.*
*Let your eyes look directly forward,*
*and your gaze be straight before you.*
*Take heed to the path of your feet,*
*then all your ways will be sure.*

*Do not swerve to the right or to the left;*
*turn your foot away from evil* (Proverbs 4:24-27).

Tell the truth and level with everything.
Look people straight in the eye,
Watch out what you are doing,
And where you are going.
Don't hang out with bums.

\* \* \*

*A man who is kind benefits himself,*
*but a cruel man hurts himself.*
*A wicked man earns deceptive wages,*
*but one who sows righteousness gets*
*a sure reward* (Proverbs 11:17, 18).

Everybody likes a kind man,
But a cruel man's got no friends.
Just people waiting to see when they can get him
Do a guy dirt, and that's what you get back.
Do him some good, and you got a friend for life.

\* \* \*

*Whoever loves discipline loves knowledge,*
*but he who hates reproof is stupid* (Proverbs 12:1).

It's good to know how far you can go and where the lines are, and to have somebody tell you what the score is if they don't get mad about it. And you're a retard if you don't listen.

\* \* \*

*Better is a man of humble standing who*
*    works for himself*
*    than one who plays the great man but*
*    lacks bread* (Proverbs 12:9).

Maybe the Pres ain't as good as you. Don't always try to be the wheel.

*   *   *

*The way of a fool is right in his own*
*    eyes,*
*    but a wise man listens to advice* (Proverbs 12:15).

If you so smart, how come you're in jail? You'd be smarter if you listen to the teach'.

*   *   *

*A wise man is cautious and turns away*
*    from evil. . .* (Proverbs 14:16).

If you're smart you will play it cool and stay away from hoods.

*   *   *

*Pride goes before destruction,*
*    and a haughty spirit before a fall* (Proverbs 16:18).

A show-off always gets slapped down,
    And Mr. High and Mighty with him.

*   *   *

*He who is slow to anger is better than*
*    the mighty,*
*    and he who rules his spirit than he*
*    who takes a city* (Proverbs 16:32).

A guy who plays it cool
   Is better off than a wheel.
     Holding yourself down
       Is better than being the mayor.

\*   \*   \*

*A man of crooked mind does not pros-*
     *per,*
*and one with a perverse tongue falls*
   *into calamity* (Proverbs 17:20).

If you are always setting up a stickup, sooner or later they are going to get you. If you are always boasting what a wheel you are, you're gonna get it soona than you think, man.

\*   \*   \*

*A foolish son is a grief to his father*
   *and bitterness to her who bore*
     *him* (Proverbs 17:25).

When you do a crime you hurt your mother and your father too.

\*   \*   \*

*He who is estranged seeks pre-*
     *texts*
*to break out against all sound*
   *judgment* (Proverbs 18:1).

Ya can always find an excuse if you get caught, only ya get in deeper.

\*   \*   \*

*Better is a poor man who walks in*
*his integrity*
*than a man who is perverse in*
*speech, and is a fool* (Proverbs 19:1).

It's better to be poor and honest than a rich liar.

\* \* \*

*Wine is a mocker, strong drink a*
*brawler;*
*and whoever is led astray by it is*
*not wise* (Proverbs 20:1).

Look out or you will end up a wino.

\* \* \*

*Who has woe? Who has sorrow?*
*Who has strife? Who has complain-*
*ing? Who has wounds without cause?*
*Who has redness of eyes?*

*Those who tarry long over wine,*
*those who go to try mixed wine*
(Proverbs 23:29, 30).

Oh boy, what a headache,
Yipes, do I feel lousy!
Man, is the old lady gonna be mad at me.
My eyes are bloodshot
I hung out in the gin mill too long.

\* \* \*

*Do not look at wine when it is red,*
  *When it sparkles in the cup*
  *and goes down smoothly.*

*At the last it bites like a serpent,*
  *and stings like an adder.*

*Your eyes will see strange things,*
  *And your mind utter perverse things*

(Proverbs 23:31-33).

Get your pincers off of that bottle of wine
  Looks good
    Goes down good—
      And if you ain't careful
        It comes up not so good.

You won't see right
  You'll think the lamp posts are movin'
    And they'll be too much shootin' your mouth
    off.

(A briefer version of this proverb: "Knock off the
  booze.")

*    *    *

*I passed by the field of a sluggard,*
  *by the vineyard of a man without sense;*

*and lo, it was overgrown with thorns;*
  *the ground was covered with nettles,*
  *and its stone wall was broken down.*

*Then I saw and considered it;*
  *I looked and received instruction.*

*"A little sleep, a little slumber,*
  *A little folding of the hands to rest,"*

*and poverty will come upon you like a*
      *robber,*
  *and want like an armed man* (Proverbs 24:30-34).


I walked by the empty lot of a lazy guy
  And by a house all wrecked up;
      And that ain't so clever,
        And what a mess they were.

The ground was covered with broken bottles
  And the fence was smashed to pieces.

When I think about it, it teaches me a lesson:
  If you sleep all day instead of doing your work,
      Before you know it you're on welfare,
        And that ain't so bright either.

\* \* \*

*If your enemy is hungry, give him bread*
      *to eat;*
  *and if he is thirsty, give him water to*
      *drink;*

*for you will heap coals of fire on his*
      *head,*
  *and the Lord will reward you* (Proverbs 25: 21, 22).

If one of the Black Hawks is hungry
　　Give him a hot dog;
　　　　If he is thirsty
　　　　　　Give him some water.

He won't be able to figure it out,
　　And you will keep him off base.
　　　　Besides, God likes it that way.

THE WORDS OF CHRIST are by far the most important resource in teaching acceptable ways of conduct in society to inner city boys and girls. Our problem is that many of the parables speak of vineyards, which are difficult for the city youngster to picture. On the other hand, something like a flour mill in the next block is very real. "Husbandman" is only a strange word, but "foreman" is a word heard almost everyday, and identifies a person that can be seen. The "road" to Jericho" is far away, but the "Mall in the project" is seen and walked on every day. The language is not disrespectful: it is used every day and is a part of life. It is real and has meaning.

The headings on some of the parables will help to explain why we paraphrased them. For example, consider the parable of the lost sheep, "The One Used Car That Was Snitched." We were talking about how a person feels when he discovers something he owns is missing, perhaps stolen. Since cars are on the minds of so many boys, and often stolen by them, we talked about stolen cars. This grew out of a natural situation that they were familiar with and, in some manner, had participated in. It is doubtful that they missed the message of how God felt when one of his children went astray or was missing.

## Don't Try to Con God

Temptations of Christ (Matthew 4:1-11)

Jesus went out by the docks and the man [the devil] tried to con him.

He didn't eat for forty days—and was starved.

After that the man came and said, "OK, if you're the Son of God, let's see you make these red bricks turn into bread."

But he didn't do it. He just said, "Cool it, man, you got to have more than bread if you want to live big."

Then the man took him to the steeple of St. Joe's. The man says, "Long way down, huh? Lots of cars too! Let's see ya jump. Don't be chicken. There's some cats with wings to catch you."

But Jesus didn't do it. He just said, "Don't try to con God, man, 'cause you can't do it."

So the man takes him to a big mountain where he could see everything and says, "Feast your pincers on that. I'll give you the whole thing if you will worship me."

But Jesus wouldn't do it. He just said, "I told you, don't try to con God. How many times have I got to tell you to cool it? You are supposed to worship God only."

So the man sees he ain't getting switched on, so he gets out of there and Jesus gets some rest.

## "They Goin' to Get God's Help"

### The Beatitudes (Matthew 5:3-11, in part)

Jesus went up on a hill. They called it a mount, and people came from everywhere to hear him. First he said,

*Blessed are the poor in spirit. . . .*

But he don't mean kids that don't have enough food or things to live on—not that kind of poor. He don't mean people who got everything goin' for them. He means people who need a push and ain't ashamed to say so. They the kind of people who need God's help to get along—and they goin' to get it.

*Blessed are they that mourn, for they shall be comforted. . . .*

This means when you are sad, and all kinds of trouble comes, God can help you. Like if your old man comes home drunk or if your mother has been out messin' around.

*Blessed are the meek. . . .*

A meek guy is the kind that don't holler and yell and get mad every time you do something. In other words, he don't bug you all the time.

*Blessed are those who hunger and thirst for righteousness. . . .*

He's not talking about food and drink, but

about people who try to do the right thing even if it don't come out right. Like when you say no more breaking into parking meters, and something makes you do it anyway.

*Blessed are the merciful, for they shall obtain mercy.*

This is a sort of "you scratch my back and I'll scratch yours" deal. Makes sense though.

*Blessed are you when men revile you and persecute you. . . .*

When the big kids pick on you, even when you know you are right, you should stick with it. Like when they want you to go grabbing a purse and beat you up if you don't. If you don't you'll be better off later.

## When a Guy Plants a Garden

The Parable of the Sowers (Matthew 13:3-23)

Jesus was hangin' around out by the lake. The people never gave him much chance to be by hisself. They came out to see him and he, bein' the kind of guy he was, didn't chase them away. So he starts to talk with them, and the crowd got so big he had to get in a boat so they won't knock him down, 'cause they all wanted to get near him. He figures out that if he tells them a story they will get what he wants to tell them, and that's better than preachin' any day. They don't like it so much when he yells, and pounds and stamps his feet.

First he tells them how things grow in the gardens that men plant over near the river. He says that a man planted some seeds near the end of his garden where the kids play ball and the kids' feet makes the ground get hard; and when the seeds start to come up they gets stomped on, and the seeds get kicked up and the pigeons come and eat them up.

Then he tells them how some other seeds get planted on top of a place where the rocks was and when the sun comes out it dries up the ground, and the seeds dried up too and they don't grow.

Then he tells them how some of the seeds gets mixed in with the weeds and the junk that's around the lot, and they don't do so hot either. That's 'cause the weeds gets bigger than the seeds, and nobody sees nothin' except the weeds.

Then he tells them about the seeds that the man takes care of by puttin' water from the river on them and pullin' up the weeds; and the kids don't steal the things that grows, and by the end of the summer the man's got somethin' to eat.

Then Jesus said, "Dig out your ears so you can hear what this story means." That means you better pay attention to this.

Then Jesus tells them what his story means, and it's very important. He says the seed is like the truth about God. He says that the ground is like a guy's brain. Then he says that the seed that gets planted and the kids stomp on, is like a guy who hears at a revival meeting and don't give a care about it.

Then he says that the seed that gets planted on the junk pile and grows and dies is like the guys that puts up their hands in the revival hall and cries and carries on, and then when they get with the gang forget all about the things about God that they heard and said they believed, but really didn't. The truth is OK—the trouble is they turned turkey too quick. And besides that, they got more scared of their friends than they did of God.

Then he gets to the real reason for tellin' this story. He says that everyone who hears what he says and thinks about it and then does his best with it everyday, no matter how many times they call him a Holy Roller, is like the seeds that the man takes care of, and they grow and gives him food. Just like all the guys that plants gardens down by the river and takes care of them. We gotta take care of what God tells us. And that's what the story that Jesus told in the boat means.

Everybody thinks that's a good story and they asks him for another one. So he tells them another one and this one's about a garden too. That's so's not to get them too mixed up.

He tells this story to show how good people and nasty people get what's comin to them and that sooner or later they all gets caught up with. Either they get a thank you or the works, for the good or nasty things they done.

Here's the story about a hood who tried a dirty trick on a guy that planted a garden. He got some seeds from a plant that was no good, and put the seeds in with the guy's tomatoes. The bad seed which was them damn burrs that grows in empty lots grew up with the tomatoes. One day the guy that owns the garden is showing it to a friend of his, and the friend says, "Hey, why don't you pull out those damn burrs? They ain't no good. They gonna raise hell with your garden!" Well, the guy that owns the tomatoes figures that if he pulls up the damn burrs he will pull out his tomatoes too, and that's no good either. So they both grew. Pretty soon the damn burrs turned brown and the tomatoes turned red, and it's time to pick the tomatoes to make sauce for pizza. So the guy that owns them first pulls up the damn burrs that are getting stuck to him and puts them in a pile and sets the things on fire. Then they can get the tomatoes without getting all stuck up with those damn burrs.

Then Jesus, still out in the boat, tells them what this is all about 'cause some of the people don't get it except what he said about its bein' a good idea to get rid of them damn burrs.

He says the tomatoes is like good people in the world. The burrs are like the hoods and bad people. The hood who put the damn burr seed in the garden with the tomatoes is like the devil who ain't never yet done a good thing in his whole life. Jesus says some day the end of the world is comin', and then everyone will get called in just like the things in the river gardens gets taken in at the end of summer. Then the good people will get put on one side, and the bad on the other. The good would go to heaven, and the bad to hell.

But there is more to the story than tellin' people that they might go to hell like the preacher in the revival hall does every Sunday. Only he don't do it so nice as Jesus does.

The rest of the story tells you that not everything is gonna be the way you want it. Even if you try to do the right thing—sometimes things don't go right. He tells them, when everything seems rotten don't give up. Anybody can give in when it's a bad day. He says to remember that when the halls in the building you live in stink from, you know what, to remember it ain't always gonna be like this. And when you ain't got enough warm clothes to go to school on a cold day, that ain't gonna last either. When things get cleared up for God's rule it will be much better, and that's what this story is about.

# The One Used Car That Was Snitched

The Parable of the Lost Sheep (Matthew 18:12)

There was a used-car lot at the corner of Main and Fillmore. The owner had one hundred heaps on it. If one of the heaps was snitched would the owner go and look for it? You bet he would. He would never give up looking till he found it.

Suppose he found it at North and Main. What would he do? Well, he would "rev it up, man" to see if it's OK. When he gets it back to the yard he would show it to the gang to have it checked out. If it checks out OK they would all be happy, 'cause that one heap is just as important as the 99 that no one stole. Well, this is the way it will be when one guy goes straight. One guy is just as important to God as 99 are who have always been OK. This is for real—God is just as interested in you as the used-car lot owner is in his heap.

GOD IS FOR REAL, MAN

## When Someone Gets in a Mess

Seventy Times Seven (Matthew 18:21-35)

Once there was a Pres of a gang, and
    One of the cats owed him some money.
        The Pres called the cat in and said,
            "Man, I want my money paid up."

But the cat didn't have any money to pay up with
    So the Pres says,
        "OK, man, you have to be slave till you
        pay up."

The Pres gave him a lot of work to do
    Cleaning out the crib
        And all the other dirty work.

The cat had an old piece, and the Pres took it
and sold it
    And kept the money.

The cat got down on his knees and asked the Pres
    To, "Give me time, man,
        I'll get the money,
            I'll pay it back."

The Pres kinda likes this cat and said,
    "OK man, just forget it
        And I will."

Pretty soon the cat meets a kid who owed him a
dime.
    The kid ain't got no money either
        And can't pay back the dime.

So the cat grabs him by the neck
And beats up on him
And stomps on him
And says, "Pay me or you'll get more."

The kid starts to cry and gets down on his knees
And says, "Take it easy, man,
I'll pay you soon as I can."

But the cat won't listen and beats on him again
And stomps on him,
Gave him two black peepers
And almost killed him.

The cat says, "Bet the next time you'll
Pay me back my dime."

The rest of the gang thinks this is a bum deal
And feels sorry for the kid
And they go and tell the Pres.

The Pres he don't go for that kinda jazz
And he sends for the cat.

The Pres is real wild now
And says, "You stupid no good jerk,
I told you to forget when *you* didn't have
any money.
How come you went up on that kid like
that?"

Well, the cat he ain't got no excuse,
But, man, is he runnin' scared now—
He knew something was comin' for sure.

GOD IS FOR REAL, MAN

The Pres is still wild
  And was gonna stomp on him
    But he gets hold of himself and just throws
    Him out of the gang.

The idea is this—
  If you don't forgive when someone gets in a
  mess that they
    Can't help,
      God won't forgive either.

It's a case of forgive—or else.

## The Cool Tenement Owner

The Parable of the King and His Servants
(Matthew 18:21-35)

One day Peter, who was one of Jesus' right-hand men, came up to ask a very important question. Maybe somebody had done him some real dirt and got him real teed off, 'cause he was mad.

He says to Jesus, "How many times do I have to forgive people when they are always buggin' me? I already did it seven times. Is it OK to take a punch at them now?" That seemed like fair enough to him.

But Jesus don't buy that and he says, "I didn't tell you seven times and then you can throw him a couple of punches. I said *seventy* times seven times."

Peter said, "What! Let's see, that's ... four hundred and ninety times!" That seems kinda rough to him, and he just don't get it.

So Jesus tells him a story like he always does when he's got somethin' to say.

The story is about the landlord who owns most of the tenements on the street, and about a guy who lived in one of them and didn't have enough money to pay the rent. The guy was behind over four months and didn't have a good enough job to get enough money to pay up, but his job was too good to get help from the welfare. So the landlord says, "If you don't pay up I'm gonna put you out and get the court to make your boss pay me what you owe before he pays you."

Well, the guy knows that if that happens his boss is gonna get real mad 'cause he don't like that kind of jazz and he will get fired. So he says, "Don't do that, man. I'll get fired, and then none of us is gonna have any money." Well, the landlord knows that this is right, and anyway he feels sorry for him and his wife and six kids. The landlord ain't such a tough guy and he says, "I'll tell you what I'm gonna do. I won't tell your boss or the judge, and I'll even forget what you owe me and we'll start all over again just like nothin' happened. Fair enough, man?" Well, the guy knows that he can never get a better deal than that and he agrees to it—and who wouldn't?

It just happened that the guy who didn't have to pay up his back rent made a loan to another guy—only five bucks and this is the day that it's due to get paid back. But the guy didn't have five bucks and couldn't pay it back. So he asked if he could pay him back next week. Well, this makes the first guy real mad and he says, "If you don't pay up I'm gonna go down to the small claims and the judge will make you pay up." And he did and the guy had to pay.

The landlord hears about this and this makes him real mad 'cause the guy that gets taken to court is a friend of the landlord. The landlord says, "OK, if that's the way you want to play I can play that way too. Now you're gonna pay what you owe me, or out you go and your pay gets to me before you." And that's just what happened.

Jesus said, "Now you remember that, the next time someone asks you to forgive him; if you don't forgive, God don't either."

## Doin' the Right Thing—Not Just Promisin'

The Parable of the Two Sons (Matthew 21:28-30)

There was a guy who had two sons. He told his oldest son to go clean up the back yard.

The son was a wise guy and said, "I ain't gonna to do it." But he really didn't mean it that way. So when no one was lookin', he went and put the rubbish in the garbage cans, and made the back yard shine.

But the old man didn't know this, so he told the young son to go clean up the back yard. So he said, "Sure, dad." But he didn't do it. He just went up to the corner and hung around.

So which guy obeyed his father?

The first son, of course.

Jesus told this story because he wanted people to know that doin' the right thing is more important than promisin' to do it and not doin' it.

Of course, the kid was wrong to talk back to his father like that. But at least it will be easy for his father to forgive him 'cause he did what he was told in the end. But the most important part is that he was sorry for what he said to his father. At least he wasn't two-faced about it. Maybe that's what Jesus means when he says that sinners will get into the kingdom of God, before someone like the younger son.

## It Don't Make Any Difference

The Parable of the Wedding Feast (Matthew 22:1-4)

The project manager's son was getting married. So his father said, "Let's throw a wild party!" So they invited all the wheels in the city. They got everything ready—beer, pretzels, pizza, 7-up, and cokes. But nobody came.

So the manager sent out some of the older kids to remind people of the party. But they still didn't come. They didn't care and told the older kids to beat it or they would call the cops.

When the manager heard this, boy, was he mad. He wanted to start a rumble right then. But he didn't. He said, "OK, to hell with them. We'll invite the people in the project—they ain't so bad." When they came the manager gave them new clothes to wear. There was one guy who still wore his own rags. When the manager asked him how come, he wouldn't say anything. So the manager had him thrown out.

This is only a made-up story, but if you take out the word, manager, and put in, God, and take out "party," and put in "heaven"—look what you got.

So it don't make any difference if you're a city wheel, or a fuz or who—it's best to do what God wants you to do.

# Fair Deal

The Workers in the Vineyard (Matthew 20:1-16)

The time came for the trucks and boats to get loaded down at the flour mill. They needs a lot more guys to put the sacks on the trucks and boats and on freight cars. So the foreman on the first shift goes up to the union hall where guys were hangin' around waitin' for a job to come along so they can make a few bucks.

The foreman makes a deal with a bunch of guys to load a big trailer truck. He said he's gonna pay them $1.25 an hour to work on his shift. So they came to work at six A.M. and worked hard loading up the truck.

About nine o'clock some other guys come around looking for a job, and the foreman says, "OK, you're on, get to work," but he don't tell them what he would pay. He just says, "I'll make it right with ya." So they started to work. About noon some of the winos that been sleeping under the old buildings got sobered and came looking for a job to get more money so they can get stoned that night, and they asked for a job. They got one, and the foreman says, "I'll make it right with ya," and they starts to work, but not very hard 'cause they are still a little sick from getting stoned the night before. They is still a lot of flour to put on the trucks, so when some big kids that goes to high school comes by after school he gives them a job and says, "I'll make it right with ya." And they likes to show everybody what big guys they is and how strong their muscles is, so they works hard and gets all sweaty. The foreman puts on some more guys just when his shift is most over and they only work for an hour. Then everything was loaded and the truck pulls out, the freight cars get their doors closed and the engine comes and pulls them away, and the boats start to send out a lots of smoke and blow their whistles like hell, and the little tugs come and the big boats goes away, too.

Now comes the time when everybody gets paid off. They get in a line and everybody is pushin' 'cause they wants to get paid first. The foreman has got their money in little envelopes to give them. Everybody is happy. The guys that was at the union hall thinks about the food they can buy, the winos is thinkin' about the wine and beer they gonna get, and the high school kids about a new pair of pants and stuff like that.

When the foreman gives out the money, everybody is got the same money—the ones from the union hall that worked all day, the winos, the high school kids, and the ones that got a job near the end of the day. This makes everybody mad except the ones that don't work so hard; but mostly the ones who worked all day started to yell and say that they was gonna start a strike, and carry signs sayin' UNFAIR.

The foreman says, "Now wait a minute, you guys—I kept my deal with all of you guys—ya got no kick comin, see! I told the first ones $1.25 an hour, that's what I paid you, right?" And they said, "That's right." Then the foreman says, "I told the rest of you guys that I'd make it right with ya and I did pretty good by ya, didn't I?" And they said that he did. "I kept my deal and I didn't do nothin' wrong, and you got no kick comin'. That's the way I wanta do it, and that's the way it's gonna be. I just wants to give the high school kids a break and help them out 'cause I like them. What's wrong with that?" The first guys couldn't think of anything except they still thinks that they are getting cheated. But they figures that the foreman kept his word and did what he was supposed to with the deal he made, and that's fair enough, but they didn't like it.

This story tells us that God can treat us the way he does 'cause of his love and not on account of how much stuff we do. Course this don't mean that you can go snatchin' purses and robbin' parkin' meters, and shop liftin'. But it does mean that God treats you good and keeps his deals too.

## If Ya Use Your Brains They Grow

The Parable of the Talents (Matthew 25:14-30)

There was this lady who liked to sing—sometimes long-hair stuff, sometimes hootenanny. Everytime she sang her songs she got better, even when she sang on the Mall in the project. Even the kids like to hear her—and, man, she got to be good for that.

Now the story gets mixed up a little—but just you guys listen. There was this guy—a cool cat kid. He couldn't sing—but man, could he drive a hot rod. At first he didn't win nothin' on the drag strip—but he kept trying—pretty soon he comes in third, then he keeps trying and he makes second. But he never made it big by getting first. But just like the lady he gets better by trying.

Get ready, man—here we go again. There is another guy—he's got brains—he's no retard—he's just a real gone kook—he don't try nothin'. So he don't get any better, he don't get worse either. It's just that nothin' happens—and he's gonna stay in the projects all his life.

Now what this say?

It says—that if ya use your brains they grow—if ya don't, brother, you've had it.

Something else too—it says God gave us brains and he expects us to use them. If we don't we lose what we got—but not 'cause God's mad at us—it's 'cause we didn't believe in ourselves and use what we got.

# A Stoolie in Jesus' Gang

The Betrayal by Judas (Matthew 26:14-25; 47-56)

Judas was a member of Jesus' gang,
> He was a stool pigeon.
>> He figures he can get some money by turning in Jesus
>>> To his enemies.

The stoolie goes over and makes a deal for thirty bucks
> And tells the other gang where he will be.

Later that night they come looking for Jesus
> With stoolie Judas leading the way.
>> He came up to Jesus and said,
>>> "Hi, boss," and gave him a kiss.

This made Jesus very sad
> And he said, "Judas, why do you turn me in with a kiss?"
>> Just then the rest of them grabbed Jesus,
>> But Peter ain't about to let them get away with that
>>> And he pulls out his blade
>>>> And, bingo, off comes a guy's ear.

Jesus don't go for that stuff
> And he tells Peter to put his blade away,
> And heals up the guy's ear and head.

They put the cuffs on Jesus and takes him away.
> He got taken to the house of a character called

Annas.
And this started a long trial.

Later the stoolie started wishing that he hadn't
done what he done
And he tried to give back the money,
But they wouldn't take it, no matter how
much he tried
To get them to do it.

The more he thunk of what he did
The madder he gets at himself.
He can't get it outa his mind.

There's no other way, so he gets a rope
And hangs himself.

This is more than feeling sorry for himself—
It's what the head shrinkers call guilt, what-
ever that is.

## The Rich Creep Has It Hard

The Story of the Rich Young Man (Mark 10:17-31)

One day a rich creep
   Came fast lamming it up to Jesus.

He said,
   "Hey, good man,
      What I gotta do to live forever?"

Jesus says,
   "Why ya call me 'good,' man?
      Only God's good.
         You know
            You're not supposed to steal
               Or rub out or lie."

"Ya, I know," says the rich creep,
   "But I still ain't got it."

But Jesus still likes the creep
   So he tells him,
      "Get rid of all your apartment houses
         And 'rent-a-trucks'
            And give lots of money to the poor.

"Then you will be happy
   And come on back
      And join my gang."

The rich creep says,
   "Ah, no, ya don't,"
      And does a slow lam out of there.

Jesus was not happy
  And said, "It ain't easy for a rich creep to get
  in heaven."

He liked what he could see better than God
  And he would always feel empty inside.

It's like the feeling you have when you skip school
  Or when you ride in a stolen car
    Or stay out late.

No, it's more like always wishing
  You had done the other thing.

# When You Ain't So Hot Yourself

Seeing the Log in Your Own Eye (Luke 6:39-42)

Can a blind kid help another blind man across
the street?
    They both might get killed, right?
        Well you're not as smart as your teach',
           But if you listen, someday you might be
           And know as much as the teach'.

Why does it bug you so much when you see
    Something wrong with another guy
        When you ain't so hot yourself?

So when you talk big, man, we say "Look, who's
talking."
    How can you help another guy,
        When you're the one who needs some help?

Why don't you wise up?
    First get yourself fixed up
        And fly straight,
           Then people won't say
           "Look, who's talking."

# A Cool Square Comes to the Rescue

The Story of the Good Samaritan (Luke 10:33-37)

A man was going from his apartment in the project to his friend's house. While he was walking, a couple of muggers jumped him in a dark place. He didn't have very much, so they took his wallet and clothes and beat on him and stomped on him—they almost killed him.

Before long a hood came by, but he didn't give a care. Besides, the cops might ask him questions, so he beat it out of there. Next came a squeak—never gave the poor guy a second look. After a while a real cool square comes along. He sees the character, feels sorry for him. So he puts a couple of band aids on, gives him a drink, and a lift in his car. The square even put him up in a room some place. Cost him two bucks, too!

So who do you think the best guy was? Well, you got the message, bud. But you don't have to be a square to show love, and to be sorry for someone, and to help a guy. But get with it, man—this is what God wants you to do.

## Throwin' a Party for Junior

The Prodigal Son's Return (Luke 15:11-32)

They was a rich guy who had two sons. Junior says, "Hey, Dad, how's about giving me my share of your dough now, why wait until you kick off?"

His father says, "OK, man," and gave him half his money. So Junior starts off to have a good time. At first, he's got lots of friends, a white Cadillac, two suits, and what he eats is real class, and beer at every meal. But, pretty soon the money is all gone and he's dead broke.

So he's got no friends, no money, no nothin'; and, man, oh man, is he hungry, and no pad to sleep in. He goes over to the stockyards to look for a job, and gets one feeding the pigs. The boss don't pay very much, and the pigs get more food than he does.

So Junior thinks this over and says, "I must be some kind of a nut. I was better off at home. It wasn't so bad at that. I guess I'll go home and tell 'em I'm sorry I made a real goof of this one."

All the time this is goin' on, Dad's thinkin' about it, too. He's plenty worried about Junior getting mixed up with queers and winos and he wishes that Junior would come home. So he watches out the window every night.

Then one day he sees Junior way down the end of the long block. Dad runs like crazy to meet him. Junior starts to tell his dad how sorry he is and that he made a goof to do what he did. But his dad tells him to knock it off and come home and get some clean rags on and we'll have a big supper. Dad's pretty happy to see the little cat 'cause he thought that Junior was dead, and that he would never see him again.

While this was happenin', the other son had stayed home and worked. He was out workin' his paper route when Junior came home. When he gets home from his papers he sees a wild party. So he says, "What gives?" Some guy says, "Your brother came home, and your dad's throwin' a party." This makes him mad, and he says, "To hell with that jazz," and won't even go in the house.

Dad comes out and tries to talk him into it. He says, "I stay home and sell papers and keep this place clean, and you don't buy me a damn thing. Junior here chickens out on his big plans and you throw a party and say 'Glad to see you home.' Well, I say to hell with him."

The old man's not so dumb and gets on to what happens here and knows that he just jealous. So he says, "My boy, you just settle down a minute. I always loved you, and I love your brother too. I thought he was a gone cat and was dead, but he ain't and I'm happy. I could always see you but him I couldn't. This party is for me, I'm so happy." That's how God feels when people come back to him.

## Be Sure You're Levelin' with God

The Story of the Judge and the Widow (Luke 18:1-8)

Sometimes it takes more than five minutes to get an answer to a prayer. Maybe a week or so. You can jive and cuss and fight, but it ain't gonna hurry up God. He wants to make sure that you are levelin' with him. Then too he wants to make sure that the things you want are for real.

This story tells you about—

A broad that don't got no husband 'cause he's dead. Had some dirty deals pulled on her by some no good-for-nothin' guys. She's too small and old to do much about it. She goes to the city court to get the guys fixed but for good.

The judge that she pulled is a bum and a crook, too. In fact he didn't give a good damn about the old broad. He didn't pay much attention to her and kept postponing the case but she kept coming back to tell him her trouble.

Before long he gets sick and tired of the dame, so he said, "Well, we might as well see what she wants and help her, then she'll get out of my life." He figures that the easy and quick way is to give her what she wants 'cause he don't give a good damn for the other guys either. Just so long as she stops bothering him and gets lost.

The lesson is this. Never give up on your prayers, 'cause if what you ask for is good for you and if you mean it, you may just up and get it.

## The Wheel and the Character

The Pharisee and the Tax Collector
(Luke 18:9-14)

There is always someone around who thinks that he is a wheel. They look down on other people and think they are sinners. To show them that they ain't so hot either, Jesus told a story.

Two men went to a church to pray. He called one a Pharisee—that's some kind of a religious nut, and the other was a tax collector and who likes a guy like that?

The Pharisee prayed so that everyone could hear. "God, I'm glad that I'm not like other men, like queers, and fairies, and people who cheat the worker from the welfare, and people like that. I'm glad I'm not like this character over here either, a no-good tax collector. Hell, man, I give 50 cents a week and give up a few meals."

The tax collector just stood up and prayed, "God, maybe I'm not so good, but please help me?"

And Jesus said, "See, it's the tax collector who God hears—not the one who is always shooting his mouth off about how good he is."

## They Were Real Important-Like

Jesus Calls His Disciples (John 1:35-51)

One day Jesus was hanging around down by
the river.
 There was some other guys who were friends
  Of a square named John.

They takes a look at Jesus and says,
 "There he is—God's man."

Jesus says, "So what's new with you?"
 They tell him, "Not much.
  But we hear you're a good Joe and we want
   To join up with you.
    Where is your pad?"

So Jesus says to them, "Come along and I'll
show you."
 And they did.
  Jesus didn't tell them how stupid they were
   Or call them retards—
    He talked to them like they were real
    important-like.

One of the cats was named Andrew.
 He liked getting this kind of treatment
  And goes and gets his brother.

His brother's handle is Simon and he is a
fisherman,
 Nobody thinks very much of a fisherman 'cause
 they stink,
  And that's for sure.

Simon listens real cool-like to what Andrew is
saying
    And he wants a friend, too, so he goes to see
        what's this about.

When Jesus sees them coming he says,
    "Your name is Simon, and your pop is named
John."
        Simon says, "Hey, how'd you know that—
        who told you?"

Then Jesus says, "I'm gonna call you Peter."
    This kinda shook Simon up, 'cause, even before
he could say a word,
        Jesus knew all about him.

So he figures out that Jesus must be God's man
    Just like Andrew says.
        And he joins up with the gang, too.

The next day they all start for Jesus' crib.
    On the way they meets a cat that they knew
        From their own turf—
            His name is Philip.

Jesus says, "Come on, join up with us."
    Well, Philip is out tracking anyway, so he
joins up.

Phil listens to what Jesus is got to say
    And figures that he is God's man, too.

Now Phil's got a friend—his name's Nathaniel.
    Phil says, "Hey, Nat baby, we found the one

That 'The Book' told was coming.
        He lives in Nazareth."

But Nat knows the Book pretty good and that God's man
    Is supposed to come from Bethlehem.

So he says,
    "You been sucked in, pal,
        Somebody is giving you a con job."

So Phil says,
    "So OK, come take a look yourself."
        And he did.

Jesus gives him the same treatment that Pete got.
    He tells Nat all about himself.

Nat's no retard himself, so he figures out that
    If Jesus knows this much and I didn't tell him anything
        Either somebody's a stoolie
            Or he is God's man.
                And Nat joins up, too.

Then Jesus says to his new friends,
    "You're gonna see some pretty big things from now on."

One of the reasons that they got to be friends
    Was that Jesus didn't blast 'em
        Or climb up on 'em.
            He just treated them like they were somebody,
                And they were friends all the rest of the time.

## Touchin' Is Believin'

The Story of Doubting Thomas (Luke 24:36-48;
John 20:19-31)

After Jesus busted outa the grave
  He met two of his gang on a road.

Man! were they ever spooked and surprised.

They ran like crazy to the place where the other
guys were.
  And started to tell who they seen.

Before they could say much, bingo!
  Jesus was there,
    Came right through the door,
      And they couldn't figure that out either.

He said, "Peace!"

Good thing to say 'cause they was plenty scared
  Knees shakin' and teeth jumpin'.
    They thought for sure, this is a ghost.
      And who wouldn't?

So Jesus says,
  "What buggin' you?
    I ain't no ghost."

"See, I got hands
  And feet just like you guys.
    Go ahead, touch me and see.
      You know seein' is believin'."

Well, they couldn't fight that; so they believed,
But, man, were they still surprised.

Just about then Jesus says,
"What cha got to eat? I'm hungry."

So they gave him some fish fry.

After supper Jesus told them about how he busted
out of the grave
And why,
So that they could get rid of their sin and all
Of the bad things they did, and some
did plenty.

He told them he wanted
Them to tell all the cats in the world
About it.

He wanted the squares and hoods,
The rocks and squeaks and collegiates to know
about that, too.

Now the guys in the room were
Pretty hep about the whole thing.
Who wouldn't be to see someone
Who busted out of a grave?

One of the Jesus gang was not there—
He musta been real beat
And was out hanging around the corner
Or maybe out tracking another gang.

He thought that the Jesus gang was all washed up anyway.

He didn't have no place to go
  An' nothin' to do
    So he went up where some of the Jesus gang were.
      Maybe they could talk over old times.

The rest of them say,
  "Well, look who's here
    Mr. Sad Puss hisself—
      Where ya been?"

"Betcha can't guess who was here."
  Thomas says, "So who cares?"

The rest of them says, "Jesus was here."

Thomas says,
  "Whats a matter with you guys,
    You trying to be funny or something?"

Well, the rest of the guys finally get it through
  His thick head that they did see Jesus.

So Thomas says, "All right, all right, so you saw him,
  But I ain't believing till I
    Touch him.
      Is that so bad?"

About a week later the Jesus gang
  Was in the same room again.

Thomas ain't takin' no chances this time,
　　So he goes to the meetin'.

Sure enough Jesus came again
　　The same way,
　　　　Right through the door;
　　　　　And they still
　　　　　　Don't understand it.

They didn't try to figure it out
　　But they still were surprised.

Thomas' eyes almost bugged out when he saw
Jesus.

He just looked and looked
　　And he says to himself,
　　　　How about that?
　　　　　They did level with me.

Jesus knows that old Thomas is having trouble
　　Believing about him still being alive.

He didn't yell at him
　　Or bawl him out,
　　　　Or tell him he was no good,
　　　　　Or swear at him.

He just walks over and says,
　　"Evening, Thomas,
　　　　I just want to help you.
　　　　　Don't be scared.

"Just touch me and you'll see I'm for real."

So Thomas did touch him
First, his hands
Then his side,
Right where he got stabbed.

That did it,
Thomas knew the rest of them was right
And he was just as happy as the rest.

Thomas says, "You are for real!
You're the Lord!"

Jesus says,
"You believe 'cause you see me.
People who believe without seeing me
May have it hard too,
But that makes it better for them."

THE WORD SALVATION was a stumbling block until we remembered the incident of a man who had been about to drown in the creek. We talked about someone in the flour mills who had seen what was happening and had then run from the mill to pull the man out of the creek. Thus, salvation became "getting pulled out." To be saved was "pulled out." It was interesting that this was associated with the act of someone else or that a person was pulled out by someone who didn't have to do it. With that thought we worked on the story of Nicodemus and, later, of Paul and Silas in the Philippian jail.

## When a Man Gets Pulled Out

Nicodemus and the Meaning of Salvation (John 3:1-21)

One night a man hunted out Jesus.
He said, "I got the feeling that you're on
the level
And you don't give us the go round."

Jesus said,
"Right, man.
Unless a man gets pulled out he will never
see God."

So Nicodemus said,
"So what do you want me to do,
Fall in the creek and wait for a cat to pull
me out?
Man! what if he don't come along?"

Jesus says,
"No, no, no,
I'm not talking about the creek,
I mean the way you're drifting, man.

You're always getting into trouble
And all that jazz.
To knock that off is what I mean."

When you're in the alley you hear the trucks.
You can't tell what street they are on
Or where they are going, right?
But the trucker knows where he's going.

That's how it is when you get pulled out.
  You act like you know where you're going
    And you do know where you're going
      And you don't drop out.

Then Jesus came right out with it and said,
  "God loved everybody
    So much that he sent his son, Jesus,
      To pull us out
        So we would always know where we
        are going."

## Some Lunch, Huh?

Feeding the Five Thousand (John 6:1-14)

One day Jesus saw a big gang of people,
So he said to Philip,
"Oh boy! How we gonna feed them all?"

But Jesus knew what to do—
He just wanted to see if Philip could get out
of a mess like that.

So Philip said, "$200 would not buy enough bread
for that gang."

Andrew tried to help. He said, "There's a boy
here who's got a lunch—five loaves of bread
and two fishes (some lunch, huh?)."

Then Jesus said, "Tell them to sit down."
And they did, about 5,000 of them.

Then Jesus took the bread—prayed over it,
And the same thing with the fish.
They gave it to the gang seated on the
ground—
And, man, there was enough to feed
everyone—and twelve baskets left!

When the people saw this they knew who Jesus was.

It was easy for them to believe
Because he could prove he was God's Son
By doing things nobody else could.

# Bad Friday

The Trial and the Crucifixion (Matthew 27: 11-54; Mark 15:1-39; Luke 23:1-49; John 18:28-40; and 19:1-30)

The wheels took Jesus up to the governor who had a funny name. It was Pilate. He didn't know nothin' about Jesus, so he took him into his big office and talked with him and asked him lots of questions. Pretty soon he comes out to the people and says, "Jesus is OK. They ain't nothin' wrong with him." The wheels don't like that, so they gets everybody to yell, "Kill him, kill him, he is causin' lots of trouble around here, and everywhere."

This guy Pilate don't want no part of this and he's thinkin' of a way to get out of it. So he says, "This man comes from another place. I'll send him over to Herod." But Jesus didn't give Herod no answers to his questions, and this made Herod mad and he says, "OK, you asked for it." He had a big purple robe put on Jesus and pokes fun at Jesus. But Herod ain't takin' the rap for this one either and sends him back to Pilate. Pilate's wife had a dream about Jesus and she tells Pilate, "You better let him go. He ain't done nothin' so bad that you have to kill him." Pilate wanted to let him go too so he told the people, "We checked Jesus out and he's OK. There's nothin' wrong with him." But the people wanted blood and they start yellin', "If you let him go you'll be in trouble with big daddy in Rome and we'll get you kicked out." Well, this makes Pilate scared so he tried to find another way out. He figures that he's got them trapped with this one. He tells them about a real big crook by name of Barabbas and says, "I'll let one go—Barabbas or Jesus—who will it be?" They all start yellin', "Barabbas." Pilate never thought that they would yell that, and this bugs him plenty. He tries once more to get out of it and says, "What shall I do with Jesus?" The crowd yells back, "Kill him." But Pilate still wants nothin' to do with the whole thing and tells one of his flunkies to bring some water to wash his hands, to show everybody he's washin' his hands of the whole thing. But like all the other politicians he wants to please everybody and he sends some of the army guys to take Jesus away to get killed. They wanted to have some fun with Jesus first, so they put a crown on his head, only it was made of thorns, and then they spit on him and beat on him and did all kinds of nasty things to him. Then the time came and they made him carry the heavy cross that they was gonna kill him on. They was two crooks gettin' killed that day too.

Everybody followed just like it was a big firemen's carnival or somethin' like that. Jesus had taken such a beatin' that he passed out, and the army guys grabbed one of the crowd to carry the cross and that was the only good thing they did all day long. When they got to the top of the hill they stripped Jesus and the two crooks and put them on the crosses and pounded nails in their hands. Then they put up the crosses and waited for them to die. The army guys sold chances on his clothes.

Pretty soon Jesus says, "Don't be too hard on them, Father, they been led on by the crowd. They don't know what the score is."

Then they put up a sign. It says "King of the Jews."

About that time one of the crooks was hurtin' real bad and he started swearin' and makin' fun of Jesus. The other crook he don't want no part of that and tells the first crook to shut up, "The guy in the middle ain't done nothin' like we have. We got what's comin' to us, but he's OK." Then he turns to Jesus and says, "Don't forget me and put in a good word for me later." Jesus tells him, "Don't worry about it—you already with me."

The real sad part of this whole horrible mess was that his mother had to watch what was goin' on. But even then he didn't forget his mother and he tells John to take care of her.

By this time it's gettin' real dark and it lasted about three hours. Then when everything was quiet Jesus lets out a real bellow and says, "That's it, it's all over," and he died. One of the army guys standin' near the grave says, "You know what I think? He *was* God's son, that's what."

# When Jesus Busted Out of the Grave

The Resurrection (Matthew 28:1-15; Mark 15:42-47; and
16:1-8; Luke 23:50-56; and 24:1-11; John 19:38-42; and
20:1-18)

After Jesus got killed, a friend of his takes the body down and puts it in a grave made out of a big hole in the cliff. Then they puts a big stone over the door and a couple of army guys to guard it, and they put some ropes on the stone just to make sure nothin' is gonna happen to the body.

Sunday morning comes, and two gals both with the name of Mary—one of them's Jesus mother—was on their way to the cemetery to make sure everything is taken care of right. They didn't know if they could get in the hole in the cliff that was the grave 'cause the army guys were there and the stone that they put there might be too big for them to push.

But they didn't have to worry. Jesus had already busted out of the grave like he said he would. This makes the army guys worried, and when they saw an angel there that didn't help much either. So they went and tells one of the wheels in the church what happened. This makes him scared too 'cause he remembers what Jesus said about bustin' out of the grave. So he pays a bribe to the army guys and says, "Tell the people that the Jesus gang came and took him away." This would make the Jesus gang look like grave robbers and everybody hated them and that would be the end of them. But it didn't work that way.

While this was happenin', the Marys get to the grave and find that all the worryin' about how they are gonna get in is for nothin', that Jesus is busted out. First they didn't get it or remember and they think that some grave robbers have been there. Then the angel tells them what happened and that everything's right on schedule. Well, they goes to get two of the other guys. They meets Peter and John and tells them what the score is and they start to run like crazy to the grave. John can run the fastest so he gets there first. Sure enough, Jesus has busted out. John who is a pretty brave guy goes right in the grave and picks up the rags that the body got wrapped in. He figures that the only way that it can get where it is, is that Jesus musta got up. So the four of them figures out that Jesus told the truth and leveled with them when he said he couldn't be killed and that he must be alive somewhere.

But he was right near there, 'cause Mary started to cry and bawl like women do when things don't go right for them. Then she heard someone speak to her. She's got so many tears that she don't see who it is and thought that it was a guard or somethin' like that. So she says, "Man, where did you take Jesus?" But it was Jesus who was talking and he says, "Mary," very nice-like.

This time she knows who is talkin' and, boy, is she happy. So she goes and tells the rest of the gang, and they was all happy too.

Then Jesus tells her that he had to go back to heaven where his father lived but that he would still be with them. But they didn't get that bit at all.

## Ever Since Then the Preachers Been Yellin'

The Story of Pentecost (Acts 1:15-26 and 2:1-47)

After Jesus takes off for heaven up in the sky the members of his gang were having supper at the crib—second-story place, that is. All day they had been standing on the street corners beating the drums and blowing the horns and giving out little books about God and what's gonna happen if you don't shape up. They were pooped, and that's one of the reasons they was where they was. The other reason was that Jesus says he's gonna send his ghost to help them start a church. They were getting a rough time from the other gangs and needed all the help they could get, no matter where it came from—ghost or no ghost.

They were all there except Judas who was dead 'cause he killed himself for what he'd done. They had the names of two guys who were tracking but they couldn't make up their minds who to take in Judas' place, so they put the names in a hat and pulled out one. His name was Matthias.

The Jews were getting ready to have a real big jive that they called Pentecost. That's sort of like a Thanksgiving Day. A real big mob shows up, about three thousand cats and debs. Then a funny thing happened. The wind blew like crazy, fire came and jumped around all over the place, and a little bit of it was right over the heads of Jesus' gang. This scared the hell out of everybody watching—you bet it did. Then Jesus' guys started to talk all kinds of language—Spanish and German and Italian and all the other ones.

That's so that everybody can know about God. Everybody that was there was surprised to hear everybody talking in another language. Some cat says, "Hey, what gives here? I thought you said these guys come from a place called Galilee. How come they talkin' like that? Some of them come from Jerusalem and they don't know what all them other languages is about neither." So they says, "Listen to them stupid jerks. They must be stoned. Bunch of winos gittin' stoned this early in the morning."

Peter says, "What's a matter with you guys? They ain't stoned and they ain't a bunch of winos. It's just that they all worked up their religion and it's pretty good for them to be so happy.

"Ain't gonna do you guys no harm to think about what you see just now and to think about how rotten you were to Jesus when he was 'round this place. You acted like he was just a bunch of dirt and a dog under your feet. You didn't even pay no attention to people who told you about him. You ain't so hot yourselves."

This makes them feel pretty low and like dirty dogs. "How can we make it up to you," they says. This ain't no phony sounding they making—they means it. They really sorry for getting mad.

So Peter and the gang tells them to feel sorry some more and then to get baptized in the water like at the revival hall, and, cripes, about three thousand of them did. And ever since then the preachers been yellin' and givin' out books on the street and buildin' churches. And there is still people who thinks that all preachers and churches is a little nuts.

## The Beggar on Main Street

The Healing of the Lame Beggar (Acts 3:1-26 and 4:1-4)

Up on Main Street there is a guy selling pencils.
    The poor guy's legs and feet are no good,
        But he don't want to go on welfare
            So he sells pencils.

Everyday he gets up there
    And sits near a vent so he'll be warm.
        He holds out his cup with the pencils.

Some people put a dime or a quarter in the cup
and don't take a pencil
    Just 'cause they feel sorry for him.

One day two men were going over to St. Joe's
to pray.
    On the way they passed the beggar and he
    yelled,
        "PENCILS FOR SALE."

These guys' names were Peter and John.
    They belonged to the Jesus gang;
        They are squares but not such bad people.

They stopped by the beggar and said, "Look
at us."
    The beggar looked up thinking—Oh boy,
        This ought to be good for a buck.

They said, "We ain't got no money to give you,
    But we got a lot of faith and we give you that."

(They were sort of faith healers like at the
store-front church.)
"In Jesus' name get up and walk."

Then the man felt his legs get better
And he did get up
And jumped around like crazy, man.

So he went with them to St. Joe's
And the other people say, "What gives?
Ain't this the beggar over on Main Street?
See, he's been faking it all the time."

But Peter and John just said to all of them,
"Cool it . . .
And listen to what we got to say.

"You monkeys know that this guy's not been
faking it.
It would have been easy for him to go on
welfare
Instead of working the streets
That's proof that he's not a fake . . . right?"

They all says, "Right, man."

So then Peter gave them the business about
religion.
He went way, way back and told them about
Abraham and the Jewish people,
How they didn't believe either—
And how the Jews killed Jesus

Even when Pilate tried to find a way to
get him off the hook.

They all said, "That's right, man, you preaching
now—
    Tell us more."

Then Peter said how God got Jesus busted out of
the grave,
    "And now he's healed the beggar from Main
    Street
        And you can see it yourself,
            So how come you can't believe in God?"

Well, that's a good question and they didn't have
    A good answer.

They began to feel sorry for all that happened in
the past
    And said so.

And all the people that listened that day
    Were sorry about what they did,
        And got pulled out.

## Thrown in the Hole for Helpin' a Girl

Paul and Silas in the Philippian Jail (Acts 16:16-40)

A bopping gang came down the street to the city
can.

The Pres and V.P.
    dragged out two guys and gave them to the P.G.

Their names were
    Paul and Silas—
        They were preachers.

They didn't do nothing but try to help a poor girl,
    And ain't that a fine thing to get in the can for?

Here's the story . . .
    Everyday the preachers would
        Go for a walk and end up at the river and
        have a
            Prayer meeting like the Salvation Army.

On the way they passed a girl—
    She would yell,
        "These preachers come from God.
            They show you how to get pulled out."

She was like the palm reader down at the corner—
    She could tell the future,
        And the creeps that she worked for got rich
        on her,
            But the Book says that she had an evil
            spirit.

Well, one day the preacher takes sorry for her
   And tells the evil spirit to scram out of her.
      Must of let out with a big yell
         'Cause the spirit gets out but fast.

Then the girl couldn't tell the future,
   And the creeps can't get any more money from
her,
      So they gets mad at the preachers.

They grabs them and pulls them
   Along the streets
      They tells everybody these preachers
         Givin' the wrong teachin'—
           In fact against the law.

The jokers gets everybody worked up
   And yellin' against the preachers
      And they didn't really know
         Why they were yellin'.

So the wheels orders the preachers
   Stomped on and to go up on em,
      Then they got put in the hole.

The preachers were by themselves in the dark,
   The stink was awful
      And they were hurtin'.
         But they didn't start to bitch about it,
           'Cause they knew that it wont do no
           good.

So they started to talk about God

And to sing gospel songs
    And talk about God's love
       And pray.

And ain't that just like preachers?
The other cons hear 'em singin'
    At first they think
       The preachers must be nuts.

Then they realize
    They mean it.

And they are happy
    Even if they did take a beatin'.

Then it happened:
    A big earthquake came—
       All the cell doors flew open
          Even the one on the hole
             Where the preachers were.

Well, the P.G. gets worried
    When he sees this and runs to the can
       From his house.

He knew that he would get killed
    If any of the cons made it out
       So he says, "Why wait—might's well get it
over with,"
          And was going to kill himself with a big
knife.

Then the preachers yell,
    "Wait a minute, man—

Hold it,
    Cool it, man!"

And boy! Was he glad to hear that.
He got a flashlight and rushed in, and all the cons
    And the preachers were there.
        So he knew that the preachers were no tough
        hoods.
            Maybe that girl was right—
                They were from God.

So he talked to the preachers and asked
    About being saved.

And the preachers tell him to believe
    On Jesus and he will be saved
        And he did and he was.

All the other cons heard about Jesus too
    And all the P.G.'s family too.

The P.G. was so happy about this that
    He took them to his house
        And washed up their cuts
            And put band aids on.

Then he gave them food
    And something to drink
        And he treated them real good.

Then there was a baptizing service.
In the morning the
    Rulers sent word to
        Let the preachers go.

But the preachers said,
    "Oh no, you don't. We didn't do nothing.
        You ain't going to get out of it this easy."

"You want us out,
    You come let us out, you put us in here.
        We are good citizens
            You put us in the can without a fair trial."

Well, this put a scare in the rulers
    'Cause they know they ain't supposed to do
    that.
        They come runnin' to the P.G.'s house
            And begged the preachers to please go.

They didn't want to start no more trouble
    So they went away.

Later one of the preachers—
    It was Paul—
        Wrote them a letter.
            It's in the Book even now—
                It's called
                    Philippians.

## Something Inside Is Bugging Me

Paul Puzzles Over the Power of Sin (Romans 7:15-25)

Sometimes I get all mixed up at myself, and something inside of me is bugging me.

Like when I say I ain't gonna do something that's no good. I do it anyway and I hate it and myself too.

So it must be something in me that's making me do it. Like when I make up my mind I won't do something bad, I do it anyway. Sometimes it seems like I can't do anything right, and there is always bad things nearby.

It's just like as if I'm two people fighting. I want to do what God wants me to do. But it's very hard.

PLAY-WRITING is sometimes a suggested activity in church school curriculum. The following plays, "How Come This World Got Here?" and "Don't Make No Difference How Much Trouble," are examples of how this method works with other than middle-class children.

The play about the Creation was done by a group of sixth-grade students during several sessions of released-time classes. Significantly, the children thought it necessary to insert a verbal fight between Gert and Sam, which at the same time expresses considerable doubt about the whole story of the Creation on Gert's part.

The play about Job represents many hours of work in the telling and retelling of the story of Job and his tormentors. Most of the children just wanted to "bust" the tormentors on the nose, and let it go at that. After all, this is their usual method of handling problems and tormentors. It was interesting to watch the children at work on this play. They seemed to derive some satisfaction that "Mr. Job" was having all these troubles. The ending seems much too simple and, it must be suspected, represents a concept that trusting God may be all right for others but not for me. For some reason we could not get beyond this type of solution.

# How Come This World Got Here?

A Play About the Creation (Genesis 1)

SAM: If you look up between the buildings what do ya see?

GERT: Sky—right, man?

SAM: Well, that's the heavens . . .

Look down, what do you see?

GERT: Cement.

SAM: What's below the cement, girl?

GERT: Dirt.

SAM: Come on, girl, get with it—what's the name of the planet?

GERT: Earth, man.

SAM: Great goin', girl, now that's the first part of creation. First, there the heavens that God made.

GERT: What comes next?

SAM: The earth.

GERT: Hey, man, how come you know about that?

SAM: I read about it in Genesis.

GERT: You what—what you talkin' about, man?

SAM: Genesis—that's the first book of the Bible, girl. Don't you know that? Just you listen, girl, your old man knows more you think he does . . . Listen now . . . Genesis means "be-ginnings."

GERT: Well, why didn't you say so instead of the fancy word?

**117** ·   GOD IS FOR REAL, MAN

SAM: 'Cause Genesis the first book of the Bible and it tells where everything comes from.

GERT: OK, man. Tell me how come this world got here?

SAM: One day God said, "Guess I'll make a world." First, it didn't look like much, just a bunch of goo like comes on the roof on hot days.

GERT: You mean like a glob of tar or somethin'?

SAM: You got the idea, girl; it didn't look like nothin'.

GERT: Just a glob, huh?

SAM: Ya, no streets, or high risers or projects, no drunks, or parks, or rivers, no nothin'.

GERT: Well, how come there got to be somethin', then, man?

SAM: God! that's what.

GERT: God that's what? What ya mean, man?

SAM: He said, "Come on, light, shine and light up this thing—and just like when the street lights come on there is the light. He calls the light day and the dark night and that's how come we got day and night.

GERT: Great, man—just great.

SAM: You ain't heard nothin yet, girl.

GERT: OK, what's next, big daddy?

SAM: Next, he made the sky and the clouds and got the water outa where the sky is. This gets called the firmament.

GERT: It gets called the what?

SAM: The firmament—ain't that a nice word? It means sky.

GERT: So we got a sky. How did the rest get here?

SAM: The next day he makes the lakes and rivers and the earth that you look down and see. There was trees, and flowers like in the window boxes. And he made the rocks and the empty lots and the fields like the kids out in the country got. That's a lot to do in just one day.

GERT: You sure you got this right, man? Who says this is true?

SAM: I told you, girl, this come from the book of Genesis.

GERT: Oh ya, that's the one you say means beginnings.

SAM: Sometimes I think there is hope for you, girl, you remember and catch on real good.

GERT: What happens next, big daddy?

SAM: Now we got the fourth day. You still with me, girl?

GERT: Don't get funny, man, I'm still here.

SAM: Two big lights get made. One's the sun and that shines in the day.

GERT: Big deal.

SAM: One shines sometimes at night—that's the moon.

GERT: That ain't all that shines at night, man.

SAM: I'm talkin' about the creation, girl.

GERT: Keep talkin'—I'm listenin' again.

SAM: Well, the stars get made, and ever since then they been shinin' just like God said.

GERT: Ain't that sumpin?

SAM: Now comes the fifth day.

GERT: Don't take no brains to figure that out, man.

SAM: This is the day when animals get made, like lions and cats and dogs, bugs and birds. There were big ones and little ones. Fish gets put in the rivers and the lakes and Delaware pond.

GERT: How about worms to catch the fish?

SAM: Don't you get smart, girl, I'm trying to give it straightnick just like it says in the book. You better shut up or I ain't gonna tell you no more.

GERT: I'm just kiddin' you, man.

SAM: This is important stuff, and I don't like kiddin' about it.

GERT: OK, let's have the rest.

SAM: Your big mouth is always gotta sound off on somethin'.

GERT: Oh, come on, Sam baby, don't get hurt. I told ya I was just kiddin'.

SAM: OK, doll. I told you about how the animals and fish gets made, but the most important of all is getting ready to get made and show up on the earth.

GERT: Tell me about it, Sam baby.

SAM: I'm talkin' about a man. God looked at

everything he made and he says, "How about all that? Not bad for a few days' work. Seems like somethin' is missing. Let's see, what did we forget? Hmmmmm, I know—we needs a man to run the thing. We can make him somethin' like us and he can give all the animals names and keep them in line." So he makes a man and gives him a name—it was Adam.

GERT: Adam . . . how come he named him that?

SAM: I don't know, he just did. Stop buttin' in. I still got more to tell you. This makes six days God's been working hard and he had enough and says that it's time to get some rest. So he made the seventh day and he didn't do nothin', just took things real slow and easy. And that's why we got a Sunday.

GERT: Geez, all that just to get a day off.

SAM: Of course not, you dope—God was tired from all his work.

GERT: You believe all this stuff—is this for real?

SAM: I might have left out a few things, but that's the way it says in the Book and that's good enough for me.

GERT: Well, I'm gonna ask my teach'—she ought to know.

SAM: It's OK with me.

## Don't Make No Difference
## How Much Trouble

A Play About the Trials of Job (The Book of Job)

There was a man whose name was Job. He was a pretty good guy. Most everybody liked him, but God liked him best of all.

But there was one guy who didn't like him. He was the devil. So the devil says to God:

DEVIL: God, you know why Job likes you?

GOD: No, why? *(But he really did know.)*

DEVIL: It's 'cause you give him everything he wants—that's why.

GOD: So . . . ?

DEVIL: If he got sick, or lost his money, or had to live on Sycamore Street he wouldn't love you.

GOD: Oh, yes, he would.

DEVIL: Oh, no, he wouldn't. I'll make a deal with you. You let me have him and I'll show you.

GOD: Don't make no difference how much trouble you send him, he's going to stay on my side, so go ahead, try.

*End of First Act*

### ACT 2

The devil worked it out so that lots of trouble comes to Job. *(Job's setting on the step of his house watching traffic go by.)*

JOB: Ah, it's a good day today—nice and warm. *(Car stops, First Man gets out.)* Wonder who that is?

1ST MAN: Morning, Sir.

JOB: Good morning.

1ST MAN: You better sit down, Mr. Job, I got some bad news for you.

JOB: What's up?

1ST MAN: Nothing.

JOB: Well, what's the bad news?

1ST MAN: Well, ah—

JOB: Yes, yes, what you trying to tell me?

1ST MAN: Well, you know all those houses you own over on William Street—they all been condemned by the city.

JOB: Oh, man, that is bad news—*(Just then another car drives up—Second Man gets out.)*

2ND MAN: Morning, Mr. Job.

JOB: Morning.

2ND MAN: You better sit down, Mr. Job.

JOB: Oh, oh, not again.

2ND MAN: What do you mean not again?

JOB: I just had some bad news from him and that's how it all started.

1ST MAN: That's right.

2ND MAN: Get ready for some more.

JOB: OK, let's have it.

2ND MAN: You know all those cows and chickens you used to own out near Cradle Beach?

JOB: What do you mean, used to own?

2ND MAN: That's the bad news—lightning killed them all.

JOB: Damn it. *(Just then the telephone rang. Job goes inside to answer.)*

JOB: Hello.

VOICE: Mr. Job?

JOB: Uh huh.

VOICE: This is the captain of your boat. You better sit down.

JOB: Oh, not again?

VOICE: What's that?

JOB: Oh, nothing—what's your bad news?

VOICE: How did you know it's bad news?

JOB: Oh, never mind—just tell me.

VOICE: You want it straight?

JOB: Yeah.

VOICE: You ain't got a boat no more. Somebody stole it and—

JOB: Well, I'll be an S.O.B.

VOICE: Me too.

JOB: Goodbye.

VOICE: Goodbye. *(Just then the door bell rang. Job goes to the door—it's a cop.)*

COP: Good morning, Mr. Job.

JOB: Now don't you start that.

COP: Start what, Mr. Job?

JOB: I got no time to gum with you, just tell me that bad news.

COP: How did you know I have bad news?

JOB: Never mind—let's have it and I'm not going to sit down.

COP: OK, have it your way.

JOB: Well?

COP: Your kids were in an auto accident with a fire truck—they are all dead.

JOB: Thanks for telling me. *(This really got to Job. So he goes into the bedroom and cries his eyes out. But he still don't blame God for all his troubles.)*

### ACT 3 SCENE 1

Devil is sitting by himself in a room thinking about Job not blaming God for his trouble.

DEVIL: How about that? Now what am I going to do? *(Looks very mean—Just then God comes into the room.)*

GOD: See, I told you—give up.

DEVIL: Nope.

GOD: Might's well.

DEVIL: Nope, I got another idea.

GOD: What's that?

DEVIL: I'm going to make him so sick and tired of life he'll blame you for everything.

GOD: You are nasty.

DEVIL: Yeah, ain't I though.

GOD: OK, let's see you try. *(But he knew it won't work.)*

DEVIL: I'm going to give him boils first, and if that don't work it's chicken pox.

*(Job's in the hospital—three men visiting him)*

VISITOR: God made you sick 'cause you are a sinner.

JOB: Aw, he did not. I ain't done nothing—it's just the breaks, that's all. *(God comes in—Job bows his head.)*

GOD: Hello, Job.

JOB: Glad to see you.

GOD: Your three friends don't know what they are talking about. I'm not mad at you.

JOB: I've always trusted you even when I got troubles.

GOD *(turning to the devil who is peeking around the door):* See, I told you so.

DEVIL: Double damn and I'll be a son of a pup.

THE END


EPILOGUE

God fixed everything up and Job was happy again, and he is known because he trusted God no matter what.

# Glossary

Beatnick: nonconformist
Big daddy or big man: chief person in an organization
Black Hawks: street gang
Bopping: fighting
Broad: girl or woman
Bug: bother, trouble
Can: jail
Cat: boy or man; rarely, girl or woman
Chicken: scared not to do what someone else suggests
Climb up on them: start a street fight
Collegiate: highest form of gang structure
Con artist: good talker
Cool: calm, conservative, slow; verb, calm down, take it easy
Crap: foolishness; dice game
Creep: independent person
Crib: home
Deb: girl member of gang, usually there for sexual purposes
Fair fight: fist fight without use of rocks or knives
Fuz: policeman
Gas: meaningless words; hot air
Gasser: person who talks a lot
Get proved: show willingness to fight
Gin mill: bar
Golden ager: senior citizen
Go up on: fight a person
Gum: talk
Handle: name
Head shrinker: psychiatrist
Heart: willingness to fight
Hep: excited
High risers: apartment houses
Hood: juvenile delinquent or person who acts like one
Jerk: despised person
Jive: big party; can also mean only pretending to do something
Joker: despised person
Junkie: narcotics user
Knock it off: stop it

Kook: person who disagrees with you
Lam: run away
Long-hair stuff: classical music
Man: almost anyone
Mr. Big: important person
Mugger: robber
Pad: home or home territory
P.G.: principal guard in jail
Peepers: eyes
Pincers: eyes
Pres: president of gang
Pulled out: rescued or saved
P.W.'s: prisoners of war
Queers: homosexuals
Retard: retarded person
Rock: hood
Rub out: remove person as by killing or injuring
Rumble: gang fight
Sounding: remark made to embarrass someone
Snow job: group of lies
Square: person not up to date
Squeak: middle position—(a) square (b) squeak (c) hood
Stickup: robbery
Stoned: drunk
Straightnick: correct
The man: could be the devil or a white man
Tail: one who follows
Teach': teacher
Teed off: angry
Tracker: gang member who looks for another gang to join
Turf: gang territory or maybe your home
Turkey: person who backs out of a fight or an act
War counselor: person who makes plan for a rumble
Wheel: important person
Wino: an alcoholic